THE OFFICIAL
BURNLEY QUIZ BOOK

THE OFFICIAL BURNLEY QUIZ BOOK

**Compiled by Chris Cowlin
and Kevin Snelgrove**

Foreword by Martin Dobson

APEX PUBLISHING LTD

Hardback first published in 2008 by
Apex Publishing Ltd
PO Box 7086, Clacton on Sea, Essex, CO15 5WN, England
www.apexpublishing.co.uk

British Library Cataloguing-in-Publication Data
A catalogue record for this book
is available from the British Library

ISBN HARDBACK: 1-906358-47-8   978-1-906358-47-1

Typeset in 10.5pt Chianti Bdlt Win95BT

Cover Design: Siobhan Smith

Printed in the UK by the MPG Books Group

Author's Note:
Please can you contact me: **ChrisCowlin@btconnect.com** if you find any
mistakes/errors in this book as I would like to put them right on any
future reprints of this book. I would also like to hear from Burnley fans
who have enjoyed the test! For more information on me and my books
please look at: **www.ChrisCowlin.com**

This book is an official product of Burnley Football Club

We would like to dedicate this book to:

All the players and staff who have worked for the club during their history.

FOREWORD

Congratulations to Chris and Kevin. A tremendous amount of research has gone into the publication. I had to do a bit of research myself for the questions on Page 20!

I'm not saying if I was 100% correct! But I've got to own up - it was a little embarrassing!

Interesting to see Adam Blacklaw's name on the League goalscorers list. That did stump me!

But what could be better for any passionate Clarets fan, returning from victory from far flung places such as Plymouth or Ipswich, than improving their knowledge of their Football Club, the history, the tradition, the players and the managers.

Best wishes
Martin Dobson

INTRODUCTION

I would first of all like to thank Martin Dobson for writing the foreword to this book. I am very grateful for his help on this project.

I would also like to thank Paul Stanworth and Darren Bentley at Burnley FC for their help and advice during the books compilation. I would like to give a special mention to Burnley's historian Ray Simpson, who has helped making sure every fact and figure is 100% accurate. Ray compiled an excellent book called *The Clarets Chronicles* that no fan should be without (published in 2007 by Burnley FC).

I hope you enjoy this book. Hopefully it should bring back some wonderful memories!

It was a delight working with Kevin Snelgrove again, who is very well organised. We have written many books together and between us I hope we have given you a selection of easy, medium and hard questions.

In closing, I would like to thank all my friends and family for encouraging me to complete this book.

Chris Cowlin.

Best wishes
Chris Cowlin

CLUB HISTORY

1. What is Burnley's nickname?

2. In which year were Burnley founded – 1880, 1882 or 1884?

3. True or false: Burnley Football Club turned professional in 1885?

4. In 1885 Burnley made their first appearance in which competition?

5. True or false: in 1888 the club was a founder member of the Football League?

6. What is the name of Burnley's ground?

7. How many of Burnley's 46 League matches did they win during 1920/1921, finishing Champions of the First Division - 21, 22 or 23?

8. Who were Burnley's first ever opponents at Turf Moor in 1883, a game they lost 6-3?

9. In the 2000/2001 season who became the first £1 million signing for Burnley on a transfer from Stockport County?

10. Who was Burnley's very first manager, in charge of the club from 1894 to 1899?

CLUB RECORDS

11. Who holds the record for making the most League appearances for the club with 522 appearances?

12. Who holds the record for scoring the most League goals for the club with 179 goals in his 316 appearances?

13. How many times have Burnley won the Division One title, the last being in 1960 – 2, 3 or 5?

14. Who scored a record 35 League goals in a season for The Clarets in Division One during the 1927/1928 season?

15. Burnley were playing which team when they achieved their record home attendance of 54,775 in the FA Cup, third round, at Turf Moor during February 1924?

16. In which year did Burnley clinch their record League victory, a 9-0 win against Darwen in Division One – 1892, 1992 or 2002?

17. Who won a record 51 caps for Northern Ireland whilst at Turf Moor, a club record for the most capped player whilst at Burnley?

18. In what year did the club record their only FA Cup final win?

19. Which cup did the club win for the first time in their history during 1978/1979?

20. Which player did The Clarets sell to Glasgow Rangers for a record transfer fee of £3.25 million during June 2008?

CLUB HONOURS

Match up the honour with the season in which it was attained by Burnley

21.	Division One Champions	1961/1962
22.	Division Three Champions	1973/1974
23.	FA Charity Shield Winners	1959/1960
24.	FA Cup Winners	1991/1992
25.	Division One Runners-up	1972/1973
26.	Division Four Champions	1981/1982
27.	Division Two Champions	1946/1947
28.	FA Cup Runners-up	1913/1914
29.	Pontins League Division Two Champions	1948/1949
30.	Central League Champions	1997/1998

MANAGERS - 1

Match up the manager with the period he was in charge at Burnley

31.	Frank Casper	1900-03
32.	John Bond	1989-91
33.	Jimmy Adamson	1976-77
34.	Alan Brown	1996
35.	Harry Bradshaw	1954-57
36.	Chris Waddle	2004-07
37.	Clive Middlemass	1997-98
38.	Joe Brown	1894-99
39.	Steve Cotterill	1983-84
40.	Ernest Mangnall	1970-76

NATIONALITIES

Match up the player with his nationality

41.	Diego Penny	Scottish
42.	Christian Kalvenes	Nigerian
43.	Steven Caldwell	Irish Republican
44.	Alan Mahon	Northern Irish
45.	Ade Akinbiyi	Dutch
46.	Clarke Carlisle	Scottish
47.	Remco Van der Schaaf	English
48.	Kevin McDonald	Danish
49.	Steve Jones	Norwegian
50.	Brian Jensen	Peruvian

MANAGERS – 2

*Match up the manager with the period he
was in charge at Burnley*

51.	John Haworth	1985
52.	Stan Ternent	1958-70
53.	Harry Potts	1910-24
54.	Frank Hill	1996-97
55.	Adrian Heath	1903-10
56.	Brian Miller	1991-96
57.	Billy Dougall	1948-54
58.	Spen Whittaker	1979-83
59.	Jimmy Mullen	1957-58
60.	Martin Buchan	1998-2004

INTERNATIONALS

Match up the player with the number of caps he won for his country

61.	Frank Sinclair	16 caps for Trinidad and Tobago
62.	Alan Mahon	1 cap for Nigeria
63.	Mohammed Camara	28 caps for Jamaica
64.	Ian Cox	9 caps for England
65.	Ralph Coates	2 caps for Republic of Ireland
66.	Chris Waddle	35 caps for Scotland
67.	Ade Akinbiyi	5 caps for Jamaica
68.	George Brown	79 caps for Guinea
69.	William Donachie	62 caps for England
70.	David Johnson	4 caps for England

JIMMY ADAMSON

71. Jimmy was born on 4 April in which year – 1927, 1929 or 1931?

72. How many decades did Jimmy's overall career span at Burnley Football Club – 2, 3 or 4?

73. Jimmy signed his first professional contract in which year – 1945, 1946 or 1947?

74. True or false: in the season of 1961/1962 Jimmy was voted Footballer of the Year?

75. How many League appearances did Jimmy make for Burnley – 426, 436 or 446?

76. Jimmy played in more FA Cup games for the club than any other Burnley player, making how many appearances – 50, 52 or 54?

77. True or false: Jimmy was included in the England squad for the 1966 World Cup?

78. Against which team did Jimmy play his last game for The Clarets in 1964?

79. How many football clubs did Jimmy go on to manage from 1970 to 1980 – 4, 6 or 8?

80. True or false: Jimmy remains the last Burnley player to captain a First Division Championship team?

BURNLEY v. PRESTON NORTH END

81.   True or false: Preston beat Burnley in both League
        matches during 2007/2008?

82.   What was the score when the teams met at Turf Moor
        during December 2004?

83.   Following on from the previous question, which
        Burnley striker scored a brace in the game?

84.   In which season during the 1970s did Burnley beat
        Preston both home and away, 1-0 at Turf Moor and
        3-1 at Deepdale – 1971/1972, 1975/1976 or
        1978/1979?

85.   What was the score when the sides met in the League
        on 27 September 2008 at Turf Moor?

86.   What was the score when the sides met in the League
        during April 2003 at Turf Moor?

87.   Which defender scored a 90th minute winning goal in
        the 3-2 away win at Deepdale during February 1998?

88.   True or false: Preston beat Burnley 5-2 at home in their
        first ever meeting during September 1888?

89.   Which French defender scored the winning goal in the
        3-2 away win during December 2001?

90.   Can you name the three scorers when The Clarets beat
        Preston 3-0 at Turf Moor in the League during April
        2001?

POSITIONS IN THE FIRST DIVISION

*Match up the season with the position in which
Burnley finished in the League*

91.	1st with 55 points	1955/1956
92.	14th with 39 points	1970/1971
93.	10th with 42 points	1948/1949
94.	21st with 27 points	1952/1953
95.	3rd with 55 points	1969/1970
96.	6th with 48 points	1965/1966
97.	12th with 42 points	1950/1951
98.	7th with 44 points	1959/1960
99.	15th with 38 points	1963/1964
100.	9th with 44 points	1964/1965

LEAGUE GOALSCORERS – 1

*Match up the player with the total number
of League goals scored*

101.	James Adamson	118
102.	Alex Elder	103
103.	Jerry Dawson	78
104.	Brian Miller	69
105.	Kyle Lafferty	3
106.	Willie Irvine	17
107.	Gordon Harris	15
108.	Ray Pointer	10
109.	Ted McMinn	29
110.	Bert Freeman	0

POSITIONS IN THE SECOND DIVISION

Match up the season with the position in which Burnley finished in the League

111.	21st with 44 points	1935/1936
112.	2nd with 58 points	1907/1908
113.	6th with 44 points	1982/1983
114.	7th with 46 points	1972/1973
115.	19th with 36 points	1946/1947
116.	15th with 37 points	1911/1912
117.	11th with 40 points	1937/1938
118.	1st with 62 points	1977/1978
119.	3rd with 52 points	1934/1935
120.	12th with 41 points	1932/1933

MATCH THE YEAR – 1

Match up the event with the year in which it took place

121.	Jock Aird made his Burnley home debut in April against Liverpool	1983
122.	Burnley were FA Cup winners	1940
123.	Burnley were Division Three Champions	1992
124.	Barry Kilby joined the board as a director of Burnley	1950
125.	Tony Philliskirk was born	1961
126.	Burnley were European Champions Club Cup quarter-finalists	1998
127.	Gordon Harris was born	1982
128.	John Bond was appointed manager of The Clarets	1914
129.	Endsleigh took over as the club's main sponsor	1965
130.	Burnley were Division Four Champions	1988

FRANK CASPER

131. Frank was born on 9 December in which year – 1944, 1946 or 1948?

132. True or false: Frank played for Blackpool Schoolboys?

133. In 1962 for which team did Frank make his professional League debut, scoring against Derby County?

134. In June 1967 Frank joined Burnley in a transfer worth how much - £20,000, £25,000 or £30,000?

135. How many goals did Frank score in his first five games for The Clarets – 3, 5 or 7?

136. True or false: Frank was Burnley's top scorer in his first two seasons with the club?

137. How many League appearances did Frank make during his Burnley career – 217, 227 or 237?

138. How many League goals did Frank score while with The Clarets – 74, 76 or 78?

139. In the 1973/1974 season Frank suffered two long spells out of the game after tackles from which two players, from Tottenham Hotspur and Leeds United respectively?

140. In which year did Frank leave as Burnley manager having taken the job in January 1989?

BURNLEY v BLACKBURN ROVERS

141. In which year did the clubs first meet in the League – 1888, 1908 or 1938?

142. How many attempts did it take before Burnley recorded their first League win against Blackburn?

143. During 1959/1960 the sides met in the League and which other competition?

144. Who scored Burnley's goal in the 1-0 home win against Rovers during March 1960?

145. Who scored against Rovers in the 2-1 away defeat in the FA Cup 5th round replay during March 2005?

146. By what scoreline did Burnley beat Blackburn at home and away in the League during 1978/1979?

147. In which season did the sides meet in the League, with Rovers beating Burnley 5-0 at Ewood Park and 2-0 at Turf Moor - 2000/2001, 2001/2002 or 2002/2003?

148. True or false: the clubs have never met in the League Cup throughout their history?

149. What was the score when the sides met at Ewood Park in the League on New Year's Day 1966?

150. In which season did the sides first meet in the FA Cup, with Burnley winning 1-0 away – 1902/1903, 1912/1913 or 1922/1923?

SQUAD NUMBERS
2008-2009

Match up the player with his Burnley squad number

151.	Diego Penny	9
152.	Michael Duff	8
153.	Robbie Blake	11
154.	Gabor Kiraly	1
155.	Clarke Carlisle	20
156.	Wade Elliott	18
157.	Joey Gudjonsson	4
158.	Alan Mahon	5
159.	Brian Jensen	17
160.	Ade Akinbiyi	12

BIG WINS

Match up the fixture with the club's high-scoring victory

161.	*v. Plymouth Argyle (home),* *League, April 2007*	**5-0**
162.	*v. Norwich City (home),* *League, April 2007*	**7-2**
163.	*v. Watford (home),* *League, December 2005*	**4-0**
164.	*v. Walsall (home),* *League, September 2001*	**3-0**
165.	*v. Wrexham (home),* *League, November 1999*	**4-1**
166.	*v. Colchester United (away),* *League, October 1998*	**5-2**
167.	*v. York City (home),* *League, January 1998*	**4-0**
168.	*v. Gillingham (home),* *League, December 1996*	**5-0**
169.	*v. Peterborough United (home),* *League, March 1997*	**5-0**
170.	*v. Barnet (home),* *League, April 1994*	**5-1**

HARRY POTTS

171. Harry was born on 22 October in which year – 1918, 1920 or 1922?

172. True or false: during World War II Harry served with the RAF in India?

173. Harry made his Burnley debut in which year – 1946, 1947 or 1948?

174. What was Harry's nickname while at Burnley?

175. How many League appearances did Harry make during his four years with The Clarets, scoring 47 goals - 155, 160 or 165?

176. To which club did Harry transfer for £20,000 in 1950?

177. In 1957 Harry went into management, his first appointment being in charge of which club?

178. True or false: in 1961/1962 Harry was manager of Burnley when they finished runners-up to Ipswich Town in the First Division?

179. Harry had two spells managing Burnley, amounting to how many years in charge – 12, 14 or 16?

180. In 1979 when Burnley was at the bottom of Division Two who replaced Harry as manager?

1970s

181.   How many of their 46 League matches did Burnley win during 1974/1975?

182.   In which season during the 1970s were the club Second Division Champions?

183.   In which position did Burnley finish in the League during 1971/1972 – 7th, 10th or 13th?

184.   Which North London team did The Clarets beat 3-2 away from home during September 1973 in Division One?

185.   Burnley were relegated from Division One during 1975/1976, along with which two other clubs?

186.   How many of their 46 League matches did Burnley win during 1977/1978?

187.   Who managed the club between February 1970 and January 1976?

188.   In which position did Burnley finish in the League during 1973/1974 – 6th, 8th or 10th?

189.   True or false: the club won the Charity Shield in 1973?

190.   How many League goals did The Clarets score in their 46 League matches during 1974/1975– 68, 78 or 88?

MARTIN DOBSON

191. Martin was born on 14 February in which year – 1946, 1948 or 1950?

192. True or false: up to December 2008 Martin is the last Burnley player to have played for England?

193. In what position did Martin start his professional playing career before moving to his midfield role?

194. Against which team did Martin make his Burnley debut on 23 September 1967?

195. During his two spells at Burnley how many League appearances did Martin make – 400, 410 or 420?

196. In 1974 Martin made his first full England debut for Sir Alf Ramsey, in an away match ending in a 0-0 draw against which team?

197. How many times did Martin play at international level for England – 3, 5 or 7?

198. In the summer of 1974 Martin left Burnley in a £300,000 transfer to which club?

199. In the summer of 1979 Martin returned to Burnley in a transfer fee worth how much - £80,000, £90,000 or £100,000?

200. In 1984 Martin moved to which club, where he became player/manager and led them to promotion from Division Four in 1985?

STEVE COTTERILL

201. In which year was Steve born – 1962, 1963 or 1964?

202. In what year did Steve take over as manager of The Clarets?

203. Which team did Steve manage between February 1997 and May 2002?

204. In what position did Steve play during his playing days?

205. To which position did Steve guide The Clarets in his first season at Turf Moor – 13th, 15th or 17th?

206. In what month during the 2006/2007 season did Steve win the Manager of the Month award?

207. Which striker did Steve buy from Sheffield United in January 2007, making it the player's second spell at the club?

208. What nationality is Steve?

209. Which striker did Steve sign from Sunderland for £750,000 in June 2006?

210. During 2006/2007 Steve guided the club to 15 League wins out of the 46 matches, leading to what final position in the League?

LEAGUE APPEARANCES

Match up the player with the number of League appearances he made for Burnley

211.	John Angus	170 (22)
212.	Ray Deakin	286 (1)
213.	Adrian Heath	331 (5)
214.	Martin Dobson	438 (1)
215.	Marlon Beresford	212 (1)
216.	Steve Kindon	110 (10)
217.	Ray Pointer	406 (4)
218.	Steve M. Davis	223
219.	Leighton James	321 (6)
220.	Ian Moore	175 (10)

STAN TERNENT

221. In which year was Stan born in Gateshead – 1945, 1946 or 1947?

222. What was the only honour that Stan guided Burnley to during his time in charge at Turf Moor?

223. Following on from the previous question, can you name the season this happened?

224. How many League appearances did Stan make for Burnley during his playing career from 1966 to 1968 – 3, 4 or 5?

225. Which team did Burnley play in Stan's first League game in charge on 8 August 1998 in a 2-1 home win?

226. Following on from the previous question, which forward scored a brace in the game for Burnley?

227. In what position did Stan play during his playing career?

228. In what position in the League did Burnley finish in Stan's first season in charge at Turf Moor?

229. Stan left Burnley as manager on 3 June of which year?

230. Which Lancashire team was Stan managing before he took the job at Turf Moor?

JIMMY McILROY

231.   Jimmy was born on 25 October in which year – 1931, 1933 or 1935?

232.   What nationality is Jimmy – Scottish, Welsh or Irish?

233.   In 1950 from which club did Jimmy sign for £8,000 to join Burnley?

234.   On 21 October 1950 Jimmy made his debut away for The Clarets against which team?

235.   How many FA Cup goals did Jimmy score for Burnley in his 50 appearances whilst at the club - 11, 13 or 15?

236.   How many League appearances did Jimmy make for Burnley – 419, 429 or 439?

237.   How many League goals did Jimmy score for Burnley – 116, 118 or 120?

238.   Which team did Jimmy join in 1963, helping them to the Second Division Championship and a League Cup final?

239.   Between 1951 and 1962 Jimmy played at international level for his country, scoring 10 goals in how many appearances – 45, 55 or 65?

240.   In 1970 Jimmy had a spell as assistant manager to Nat Lofthouse at which club?

2007/2008

241. In what position did Burnley finish in the League – 3rd, 13th or 23rd?

242. Who was in charge at the start of the season as manager of The Clarets but left in November 2007?

243. Which team did Burnley play on Boxing Day 2007, with the game finishing in a 1-1 draw?

244. Which team did Burnley beat on the opening day of the season, a 2-1 home win with Mike Duff and Andy Gray scoring?

245. Against which London team did Andy Gray score a brace in a 3-1 away win during December 2007?

246. Which on-loan striker scored a hat-trick for The Clarets during the 4-2 away win against Queens Park Rangers during February 2008?

247. Which Scottish defender did Burnley sign from Preston North End during August 2007?

248. Who was the only player to appear in all 46 League matches during the season, with 45 starts and 1 substitute appearance?

249. Which manager took over at Turf Moor on 22 November 2007 from caretaker boss Steve Davis?

250. Which Scottish forward finished as Burnley's highest League scorer with 11 goals in 25 games during this season?

LEIGHTON JAMES

251. Leighton was born on 16 February in which year – 1953, 1955 or 1957?

252. Where was Leighton born – Cardiff, Swansea or Neath?

253. Leighton turned professional at what age – 16, 17 or 18?

254. On 21 November 1970 Leighton made his debut for Burnley in a 2-1 home win against which team?

255. How many League appearances did Leighton make for The Clarets, scoring 66 League goals – 336, 341 or 346?

256. In 1975 Leighton transferred to which club for a Burnley record fee at the time of £310,000?

257. After his second spell at Turf Moor in 1980 Leighton moved to Swansea City, which was under whose management?

258. In 1971 Leighton made his first international appearance for Wales against which country?

259. How many international appearances did Leighton make for Wales, scoring 10 goals – 50, 54 or 58?

260. How many spells did Leighton have at Turf Moor?

BURNLEY v. BLACKPOOL

261.   What was the score when the sides met in the League at Turf Moor on 16 September 2008?

262.   Following on from the previous question, can you name The Clarets' scorers?

263.   In which year did the clubs first meet each other in the League – 1897, 1907 or 1917?

264.   True or false: Burnley beat Blackpool at home and away in the League during 1993/1994?

265.   In which competition did the sides meet during September 2002?

266.   Following on from the previous question, what was the score in the game – 3-0 to Burnley, 4-0 to Burnley or 4-0 to Preston?

267.   Can you name the two Burnley players that scored against Blackpool in a 2-1 away win during April 1994?

268.   Which team won both League matches during 1966/1967, with a 1-0 scoreline at home and a 2-0 scoreline away?

269.   Who scored Burnley's equaliser in a 1-1 away match at Bloomfield Road during March 2000?

270.   Which midfielder scored the only goal for The Clarets in the 1-0 home win in the League during November 1999?

WHO AM I? – 1

271.   I was born in Leyland in 1933, I signed for Burnley in April 1951, I made 300 League appearances for the club, scoring 67 goals.

272.   I started my professional career at Blackburn. I played as left back for Jimmy Adamson.

273.   I made my debut in 1958/59, scoring a goal in a home win against Leeds United.

274.   I was in Burnley's first ever League Championship team in 1921. I also played for Sunderland and Huddersfield Town.

275.   I was born on 9 May 1957 in Bangor. I played for The Clarets from 1979 to 1984, making 200 League appearances and scoring 58 League goals.

276.   I was known at the Bedlington Terrier. I came to Burnley as a junior in 1959 and signed as a professional in 1961. At the age of 19 I made my first team debut against West Bromwich Albion in 1963.

277.   I was born in Leicester in 1962, I signed for Burnley in June 1984, I made 202 League appearances for the club, scoring 27 goals, I was released in May 1991.

278.   I was born in 1939, I made 202 League appearances for the club, scoring 79 goals. I then signed for Blackpool in March 1965.

279.   I made 211 League appearances for the club, scoring 6 goals. I left for Dundee in August 1960.

280.   I made my debut for Burnley against Southampton in 1967. At 21 I was appointed captain in my second season at the club.

1980s

281. Who managed Burnley between July 1986 and January 1989?

282. In which season did the club win the Third Division title – 1980/1981, 1981/1982 or 1982/1983?

283. Following on from the previous question, how many games did The Clarets win during the 46 League matches?

284. Which player did Burnley sign from Cambridge during November 1988, who went on to make 181 League starts and 1 substitute appearance in his Clarets career?

285. In what position did Burnley finish in the Fourth Division during 1985/1986?

286. Who managed Burnley between June and October 1985?

287. In what position did Burnley finish in the Fourth Division during 1987/1988?

288. Which defender signed for Birmingham in June 1986 having played for Burnley since November 1979?

289. When Mike Phelan left Turf Moor which team did he join in July 1985?

290. Who managed Burnley between August 1984 and May 1985?

ANDY PAYTON

291. Andy was born on 23 October in which year – 1963, 1965 or 1967?

292. From which team did Andy join Burnley on 16 January 1998?

293. Against which team did Andy make his Burnley debut away on 17 January 1998?

294. In Stan Ternent's first season as manager with The Clarets Andy was top scorer in all competitions with how many goals – 23, 25 or 27?

295. True or false: in the 1999/2000 season Andy won the Second Division Golden Boot award, scoring 27 goals in all competitions?

296. How many League appearances did Andy make in his five years at Burnley – 156, 166 or 176?

297. How many League goals did Andy score for The Clarets – 67, 69 or 71?

298. In January 2003 Andy played his final Burnley home game of the season, against which team in an FA Cup 3rd round replay?

299. How many League goals did Andy score for Burnley during 1998/1999 in his 39 starts and 1 substitute appearance?

300. In November 1991 which club paid £750,000 for Andy?

2006/2007

301. Which London club did Burnley beat 2-0 at Turf Moor on the opening day of the season?

302. Following on from the previous question, who scored both goals for The Clarets in the game?

303. Which defender signed from Sunderland during January 2007?

304. How many League games did Burnley win out of their 46 matches over the season – 15, 18 or 21?

305. Who was The Clarets' manager during this season?

306. Can you name the four players that scored in the 4-0 home win against Plymouth Argyle during April 2007?

307. Who scored the winner against West Bromwich Albion in the 87th minute in the 3-2 home win during April 2007, despite being 2-0 down after 8 minutes?

308. Which East Anglian team did Burnley beat 4-1 away from home during October 2006, with James O'Connor, Andy Gray (2) and Alan Mahon scoring?

309. Andy Gray finished as the club's highest League scorer with how many goals in his 34 starts and 1 substitute appearance?

310. True or false: Burnley were unbeaten in all seven League games during April 2007?

JOHN CONNELLY

311. John was born on 18 July in which year – 1934, 1936 or 1938?

312. Where was John born – Salford, St Helens or Wigan?

313. In November 1956 John joined Burnley from which club?

314. How many League goals did John score in the Championship season of 1959/1960 - 18, 20 or 22?

315. True or false: John scored the winning goal for Burnley against Manchester City at Maine Road on 2 May 1960?

316. From 1956 to 1964 how many League appearances did John make for The Clarets – 205, 210 or 215?

317. In his eight seasons at Burnley how many League goals did John score – 83, 85 or 87?

318. In April 1964 John was transferred for £56,000 to which club?

319. Which was the last club John played for before he retired from the game in 1973?

320. John also played at international level for England, making 20 appearances for his country and scoring how many goals – 7, 9 or 11?

MATCH THE YEAR – 2

Match up the event with the year in which it took place

321.	Graham Branch signed from Stockport County	2008
322.	Wade Elliott signed for The Clarets from Bournemouth	1921
323.	The club were Division One Runners-up	1960
324.	The club were Division One Champions	1998
325.	Remco Van der Schaaf was born	1920
326.	Clarke Carlisle signed for Burnley from Watford	1962
327.	The club were Division One Champions	1979
328.	The club were FA Cup Runners-up	2007
329.	The club were Division One Runners-up	2005
330.	Diego Penny made his Burnley debut	1947

TOMMY CUMMINGS

331. Tommy was born on 12 September in which year – 1926, 1928 or 1930?

332. Tommy made his debut on 18 December 1948 for Burnley away at which club?

333. In what position did Tommy play?

334. How many League goals did Tommy score in his Burnley career?

335. Which number shirt did Tommy wear for Burnley during 1949/1950 in his 41 League appearances?

336. Tommy only scored three League goals for The Clarets, in how many League appearances – 434, 444 or 454?

337. On 22 August 1962 Tommy played his last game for the club in a 2-2 draw against which team?

338. In the summer of 1967 which club appointed Tommy as manager?

339. True or false: Tommy succeeded Jimmy Hill as Chairman of the Professional Footballers' Association in 1961?

340. Tommy won three England 'B' caps, but how many full England international caps did he gain?

2008/2009

341. True or false: Burnley lost their first three League games of the season?

342. Which midfielder scored a brace in the 2-0 home win against Norwich City during November 2008?

343. Can you name the three goalscorers in the 3-1 home win against Preston North End during September 2008?

344. Who scored the only goal in the 1-0 home win against Reading during October 2008?

345. Which Northern Irish forward scored a brace in the 3-0 home win in the League Cup 2nd round against Oldham Athletic during August 2008?

346. Which team did The Clarets beat 2-1 away from home during September 2008?

347. Following on from the previous question, who scored a brace in the game for Burnley?

348. Which Premier League London based team did Burnley beat 1-0 at home in the League Cup 3rd round?

349. Who scored the winning goal for Burnley in the 3-2 home win against Watford, having been 2-1 down in the match during September 2008?

350. Which team did The Clarets beat 3-1 away from home on 21 October 2008?

HAT-TRICKS

Match up the player with the game in which he scored a hat-trick

351. Steve Kindon — v. Everton,
3 December 1949 (home), 5-1

352. Willie Irvine — v. Middlesbrough,
30 August 1975 (home), 4-1

353. Peter McKay — v. Aston Villa,
26 November 1966 (home), 4-2

354. Peter Noble — v. Liverpool,
12 April 1930 (home), 4-1

355. Harry Potts — v. Nottingham Forest,
21 February 1970 (home), 5-0

356. George Beel — v. Fulham,
2 March 1912 (home), 5-1

357. Jimmy Ross — v. Portsmouth,
19 November 1955 (home), 3-0

358. Louis Page — v. Leicester Fosse,
15 January 1898 (home), 4-0

359. Andy Lochhead — v. West Ham United,
17 November 1923 (home), 5-1

360. Bert Freeman — v. Nottingham Forest,
26 March 1966 (home), 4-1

OWEN COYLE

361. In what year was Owen appointed Burnley manager?

362. Owen was born in Scotland but was an international for which country, winning one cap?

363. In which year was Owen born – 1964, 1965 or 1966?

364. To what position in the Championship did Owen guide Burnley in his first season at Turf Moor?

365. Which team did Owen face in his first game in charge at Turf Moor?

366. Following on from the previous question, what was the score in that game?

367. In what position did Owen play during his playing career?

368. For which Scottish team did Owen play between 1990 and 1993?

369. Which Scottish club did Owen manage between 2005 and 2007?

370. What is Owen's 'saintly' middle name?

ADAM BLACKLAW

371. Adam was born on 2 September in which year – 1935, 1937 or 1939?

372. Where was Adam born – Aberdeen, Edinburgh or Glasgow?

373. In what position did Adam play?

374. Adam made his home debut for Burnley on 22 December 1956 in a 6-2 win against which club?

375. Following on from the previous question, which Burnley manager handed Adam his debut?

376. How many League appearances did Adam make for The Clarets – 318, 328 or 338?

377. Which club signed Adam from Burnley in the summer of 1967?

378. Adam made his full Scottish international debut in June 1963 against which country?

379. How many full Scottish caps did Adam win – 3, 6 or 9?

380. Adam retired from League football in which year – 1969, 1971 or 1973?

LEAGUE GOALSCORERS – 2

Match up the player with the total number of League goals scored

381.	Peter Noble	85
382.	Martin Dobson	66
383.	Leighton James	1
384.	John Angus	0
385.	John Connelly	6
386.	Billy Hamilton	4
387.	Adam Blacklaw	63
388.	Ian Wright	63
389.	Andrew Cole	58
390.	John Oster	4

IAN BRITTON

391. Ian was born on 19 May in which year – 1950, 1952 or 1954?

392. Where was Ian born – Dundee, Livingston or Stirling?

393. How many League goals did Ian score for The Clarets in his career - 8, 10 or 12?

394. Ian made his debut for Burnley on 23 August 1986, against which club?

395. How many League appearances did Ian make for The Clarets – 100, 104 or 108?

396. True or false: Ian helped Dundee United achieve the Scottish Premier League title in 1983?

397. In May 1988 Ian played his first ever game at Wembley in the Sherpa Van Trophy final, against which team?

398. In May 1989 Ian played his last home game for The Clarets, against which team?

399. True or false: Ian won the Fourth Division Championship with Blackpool in 1985?

400. True or false: Ian retired completely from the game in 1989?

1990s

401. How many managers did Burnley have during the 1990s?

402. Following on from the previous question, can you name three of them?

403. In what position did Burnley finish in the League during 1992/1993?

404. Which Essex-based team did Burnley beat 5-1 at home during December 1994 in the League?

405. From which team did Burnley sign Gordon Armstrong in August 1998?

406. In what position did Burnley finish in the League during 1995/1996?

407. Who was the club's highest League scorer with 16 goals during 1997/1998?

408. To which club did Burnley sell David Eyres in October 1997?

409. In what position did Burnley finish in the League during 1998/1999?

410. Which defender signed for The Clarets from Sunderland during August 1997 for £200,000?

WILLIE IRVINE

411. Willie was born on 18 June in which year – 1941, 1943 or 1945?

412. What nationality is Willie – Irish, Scottish or English?

413. Willie made his debut in an away match for Burnley on 11 May 1963, against which team?

414. Willie spent six seasons at Turf Moor, making how many League appearances – 126, 136 or 146?

415. How many League goals did Willie score for The Clarets, his best season being 1965/1966 when he scored 29 – 74, 76 or 78?

416. Willie broke his leg in an FA cup tie on 31 January 1967, with Burnley losing 2-1 to which team?

417. In March 1968 Willie was transferred to which club for £45,000?

418. Willie played at international level for his country 23 times, scoring how many goals – 8, 10 or 12?

419. In December 1972 Willie moved to his last League club - but which one?

420. In January 1973 Willie score his 133rd and last ever League goal, against which team?

RALPH COATES

421. In which year was Ralph born in Hetton-le-Hole – 1946, 1947 or 1948?

422. Against which team did Ralph score his first Burnley goal, away from home during March 1965?

423. How many League goals did Ralph score in his Burnley career – 24, 25 or 26?

424. In what year did Ralph arrive at Turf Moor as an apprentice?

425. Against which team did Ralph make his debut in December 1964 at Turf Moor?

426. For which team did Ralph sign when he left Burnley?

427. How many League appearances did Ralph make for The Clarets – 216, 316 or 416?

428. How many England caps did Ralph win, his first cap coming in 1970?

429. How many League goals did Ralph score for Burnley during 1967/1968, his highest tally in a season while at the club?

430. For which London team did Ralph play between 1978 and 1980?

BRIAN MILLER

431.   Brian was born on 19 January in which year – 1935, 1937 or 1939?

432.   Where was Brian born – Burnley, Blackburn or Barnsley?

433.   In what position did Brian play?

434.   Brian made his Burnley debut on 1 February 1956 in the FA Cup away to which club?

435.   How many League appearances did Brian make whilst at Burnley - 359, 369, 379?

436.   Brian played at full international level for England, making how many appearances for his country – 1, 3 or 5?

437.   How many League goals did Brian score whilst at Burnley?

438.   Which club did Brian move to from Burnley?

439.   In 1979 whom did Brian replace as manager of Burnley?

440.   In 1989 what position did Brian take up at Turf Moor?

2005/2006

441. Who was the Burnley manager during this season?

442. Which Guinean defender left Turf Moor in June 2005 for Celtic on a free transfer?

443. Which striker scored 12 League goals in 29 starts and was the club's top League scorer during this season?

444. Which Irish midfielder was the only Burnley player to play in all 46 League matches, scoring three goals?

445. Which Midlands team did Burnley beat 4-0 at home during August 2005, with Garreth O'Connor, Wayne Thomas and Ade Akinbiyi (2) scoring?

446. In which position in the League did Burnley finish – 7th, 17th or 29th?

447. Can you name the two scorers in the 2-0 home win against Norwich City during March 2006?

448. Which defender signed for Burnley in August 2005 from Sheffield United, having initially signed on loan three days earlier?

449. Can you name the two teams that finished the season as champions and runners-up, both winning promotion to the Premier League?

450. Who scored Burnley's equaliser in the 89th minute in the 3-3 home draw against Cardiff City during September 2005?

WHEN WE WERE KNOCKED OUT OF THE FA CUP

Match up the FA Cup fixture with the final score

451.	13 January 1912, 1st round	**Watford 2-0 Burnley**
452.	4 March 1933, 6th round	**Coventry City 3-0 Burnley**
453.	9 March 2003, 6th round	**Sheffield Wednesday 5-0 Burnley**
454.	16 March 1983, 6th round replay	**Tottenham Hotspur 3-1 Burnley**
455.	5 May 1962, final	**Blackburn Rovers 3-1 Burnley**
456.	29 March 1924, semi-final	**Arsenal 2-0 Burnley**
457.	8 March 1952, 6th round	**Burnley 0-1 Manchester City**
458.	8 January 2000, 4th round	**Aston Villa 3-0 Burnley**
459.	11 February 1950, 5th round	**Notts County 2-1 Burnley**
460.	31 January 1891, 2nd round	**Fulham 2-1 Burnley**

2004/2005

461.   Which Jamaican midfielder scored Burnley's first League goal of the season, in a 1-1 home draw against Sheffield United during August 2004?

462.   Robbie Blake left for Birmingham City in January 2005, but how much did The Blues pay The Clarets for him - £1 million, £1.25 million or £1.5 million?

463.   From which club did James O'Connor sign to join The Clarets during October 2004 (on loan) and then permanently in March 2005?

464.   True or false: the club qualified for the play-offs and lost to West Ham United in the semi-finals?

465.   Robbie Blake was Burnley's highest scorer during this season, with how many League goals in his 24 starts?

466.   Which Welsh goalkeeper signed for the club from Leicester City in July 2004?

467.   In what position did Burnley finish in the League – 3rd, 13th or 23rd?

468.   Who was the Burnley manager during this season, his first term in charge at the club?

469.   Can you name Burnley's three scorers in the 3-1 home win against Watford during April 2005?

470.   Who scored a brace in the 2-0 home win against Preston during December 2004?

RAY POINTER

471. Ray was born on 10 October in which year – 1934, 1936 or 1938?

472. On 5 October 1957 Ray made his Burnley debut away against which club?

473. In what position did Ray play?

474. In the 1958/1959 season Ray was the club's top League goalscorer, with how many goals – 27, 29 or 31?

475. Against which Lancashire based team did Ray score a brace in a 3-1 home League win during March 1959 with Jimmy Robson scoring the other goal?

476. How many full international appearances did Ray make for his country – 1, 3 or 5?

477. How many League appearances did Ray make for The Clarets – 220, 223 or 226?

478. How many League goals did Ray score during his Burnley career – 114, 116 or 118?

479. In August 1965 Ray was transferred to which club for £8,000?

480. How many League goals did Ray score for Burnley in his first season during 1957/1958 at Turf Moor having made 22 appearances?

BURNLEY v. BURY

481. Who scored a brace for Burnley in the 2-0 away win when the clubs met in the League Cup 1st round during August 2008?

482. What was the score when Burnley beat Bury in a League match at home during January 1997?

483. Following on from the previous question, can you name the Burnley scorers in the game?

484. Can you name the striker who scored the winning goal in the 3-2 League Cup 1st round game during August 2004 at Gigg Lane?

485. In which competition did the sides meet at Gigg Lane during January 1956, with Burnley winning 1-0?

486. Who scored the equaliser for The Clarets in the 1-1 away draw during August 1998 in the League Cup?

487. In which competition did the sides meet during 2004/2005 – League Cup, FA Cup or Football League Trophy?

488. Following on from the previous question, can you recall the score in the game at Gigg Lane?

489. True or false: the clubs first met in the League during September 1895 and Burnley won 3-0 at home?

490. Who scored a last-minute equaliser for The Clarets in the 2-2 home draw during March 2000 in the League?

ANDY LOCHHEAD

491. Andy was born on 9 March in which year – 1939, 1941 or 1943?

492. In which year did Andy sign as a professional?

493. Andy made his Burnley debut on 30 August 1960 at home, against which club?

494. On 24 April 1965 and again on 25 January 1966 Andy hit five goals in Division One (6-2) and FA Cup (7-0) matches, both at home, against which teams?

495. Andy scored his 100th League goal for the club on the last day of the 1967/1968 season in a 3-0 home win, against which team?

496. How many League appearances did Andy make for The Clarets – 226, 236 or 246?

497. How many League goals did Andy score for Burnley?

498. How many League goals did Andy score for Burnley during 1964/1965 in his 38 appearances?

499. Andy suffered relegation twice during his career, with which two clubs?

500. In which year did Andy leave Turf Moor - 1966, 1968 or 1970?

DIVISION THREE CHAMPIONS
– 1981/1982

501.   Which goalkeeper was Burnley's number 1 during the season?

502.   Who was The Clarets' manager during this season?

503.   Who scored a brace in the 3-2 away win during November 1981, with Kevin Young scoring the other Burnley goal?

504.   Which southern-based team did Burnley beat 3-0 at home on 27 February 1982?

505.   True or false: Burnley lost their first League match of the season to Gillingham?

506.   How much did a home match-day programme cost during this season?

507.   True or false: Burnley won the championship by goal difference?

508.   Following on from the previous question, who were runners-up in the League?

509.   How many of their 46 League matches did Burnley win – 20, 21 or 22?

510.   Which team did Burnley beat 1-0 in their second League match of the season at home, with Martin Dobson scoring the only goal?

WILLIE MORGAN

511.   Willie was born on 2 October in which year – 1944, 1946 or 1948?

512.   What nationality is Willie – Welsh, Irish or Scottish?

513.   How many League goals did Willie score for Burnley during 1963/1964 in his 25 appearances - 4, 6 or 8?

514.   Willie made his Burnley debut on 23 April 1963 in a 1-0 away win at which club?

515.   Against which club did Willie score a brace in a 6-1 home win on Boxing Day 1963?

516.   How many League appearances did Willie make for Burnley – 186, 196 or 206?

517.   How many League goals did Willie score during his career with The Clarets?

518.   In August 1968 Willie was transferred from Burnley to which club for a fee of £117,000?

519.   Following on from the previous question, which player took over Willie's position at Turf Moor?

520.   True or false: Willie played for his country in the 1974 World Cup in West Germany?

DEBUTS

Match up the fixture with the player who made his debut in the game

521. *v. Stoke City (home),*
    League, 0-1, January 2007   **Graham Branch**

522. *v. Sheffield United (home),*
    League, 1-1, August 2004   **Kevin McDonald**

523. *v. Sheffield Wednesday (away),*
    League, 1-4, August 2008   **Joey Gudjonsson**

524. *v. Colchester United (away),*
    League, 3-2, September 2007   **Ian Moore**

525. *v. Bury (away),*
    League Cup, 2-0, August 2008   **Wade Elliott**

526. *v. Scunthorpe United (away),*
    League, 0-2, August 2007   **Mike Duff**

527. *v. Crewe (away),*
    League, 1-2, August 2005   **Diego Penny**

528. *v. Bristol Rovers (away),*
    League, 0-1, January 1998   **Graham Alexander**

529. *v. Walsall (home),*
    League, 0-0, January 1999   **Andy Payton**

530. *v. Norwich City (home),*
    League, 2-0, November 2000   **Clarke Carlisle**

DAVE THOMAS

531. Dave was born on 5 October in which year – 1946, 1948 or 1950?

532. How many goals did Dave score for Burnley during 1968/1969 in his 37 starts and 2 substitute appearances - 3, 4 or 5?

533. Dave made his Burnley debut on 13 May 1967 at home, against which club?

534. Which former England manager said that Dave was the "finest talent in Britain and possibly Europe" when his impressive skills helped Burnley defeat Leeds United 5-1?

535. Dave spent seven seasons at Turf Moor, making how many League appearances – 157, 167 or 177?

536. To which club did Dave transfer for £165,000 in the 1972/1973 season?

537. True or false: following on from the previous question, in 1973 Dave won the 2nd Division Championship with his new club?

538. Dave won his first England cap in a 3-0 win against Czechoslovakia at Wembley in 1973, when he came on as a substitute for which player?

539. How many appearances did Dave make for England?

540. In which country did Dave have a short spell playing football in 1981?

LEAGUE GOALSCORERS – 3

Match up the player with the total number of League goals scored

541.	Jason Hardy	37
542.	John Spicer	28
543.	Graham Branch	1
544.	Andy Gray	1
545.	Frank Sinclair	4
546.	Richard Chaplow	2
547.	Dean West	10
548.	Mark McGregor	17
549.	Ian Moore	5
550.	John Mullin	7

JOHN ANGUS

551.   John was born on 2 September in which year – 1936,
        1938 or 1940?

552.   In what year did John sign as a professional on his
        seventeenth birthday?

553.   John made his Burnley debut on 3 September 1956 in
        a 2-1 home win against which club?

554.   What shirt number did John wear while playing for
        Burnley during 1959/1960?

555.   How many League appearances did John make for The
        Clarets – 419, 429 or 439?

556.   How many League and Cup goals did John score for
        Burnley?

557.   In October 1964 John scored a brace for Burnley in a
        3-2 away defeat to which club?

558.   In 1961 John played his one and only full
        international for England away to which country?

559.   For which club did John play after his career with
        Burnley finished?

560.   In what year did John retire from the game?

2003/2004

561. Who was the club's highest League scorer, with 19 goals in his 44 starts and 1 substitute appearance?

562. Burnley's first win came in their fourth match, defeating which team 3-0 away during August 2003?

563. In which position did The Clarets finish in the League – 9th, 14th or 19th?

564. Which striker scored the winning goal in the 3-2 home win against Sheffield United during December 2003?

565. Who scored a brace when Burnley beat Bradford 4-0 at home during September 2003?

566. Which defender signed for Burnley from Manchester United during August 2003?

567. Who scored the only Burnley goal in the 1-0 home win against Derby County during April 2004?

568. Who was manager of Burnley during this season, his last season in charge at the club?

569. Which East Anglian-based team did Burnley beat 4-2 at Turf Moor during February 2004, with Glen Little, David May, Richard Chaplow and Robbie Blake scoring for The Clarets?

570. Which French defender left Turf Moor during February 2004 and signed for Queens Park Rangers?

BRIAN FLYNN

571. Brian was born on 12 October in which year – 1953, 1955 or 1957?

572. Where was Brian born – Porthcawl, Porthmadog or Port Talbot?

573. Which boys club did Brian play for in Wales?

574. Brian made his Burnley debut away on 2 February 1974 against which club?

575. How many League appearances did Brian make for The Clarets – 202, 212 or 222?

576. In November 1977 which team did Brian join for £175,000?

577. In 1992 Brian was managing which team when they went on to beat Arsenal in the FA Cup 3rd round?

578. How many spells at Turf Moor did Brian have at Burnley?

579. Brian won how many caps while playing for Wales – 60, 63 or 66?

580. How many League goals did Brian score for Burnley in his career - 19, 21 or 23?

UNUSUAL RESULTS

Match up the fixture with the final score

581. v. Crystal Palace (away),
      League, May 2008   3-5

582. v. Plymouth (home),
      League, April 2007   4-7

583. v. Cardiff City (home),
      League, September 2005   5-0

584. v. Ipswich Town (away),
      League, October 2003   3-3

585. v. Preston North End (away),
      League, December 2003   5-6

586. v. Norwich City (home),
      League, April 2004   0-5

587. v. Grimsby Town (away),
      League, October 2002   1-6

588. v. Watford (home),
      League, April 2003   2-7

589. v. Sheffield Wednesday (home),
      League, April 2003   3-5

590. v. Wrexham (home),
      League, November 1999   4-0

WHEN WE WERE KNOCKED OUT OF THE LEAGUE CUP

Match up the League Cup fixture with the final score

591.   9 October 1984, 2nd round   Burnley 0-1
                                             Portsmouth

592.   9 September 1970, 2nd round   Burnley 0-2
                                             Manchester
                                             United

593.   25 September 2007, 3rd round   Leeds United 4-0
                                             Burnley

594.   5 October 1994, 2nd round   Stoke City 2-0
                                             Burnley

595.   25 October 1977, 3rd round   Burnley 1-2
                                             Charlton Athletic

596.   27 August 1991, 1st round   Aston Villa 2-0
                                             Burnley

597.   24 September 1997, 2nd round   Burnley 0-3
                                             Manchester
                                             United

598.   24 September 1996, 2nd round   Burnley 2-3
                                             Wigan Athletic

599.   6 September 1972, 2nd round   Burnley 1-4
                                             Liverpool

600.   3 December 2002, 4th round   Burnley 1-2
                                             Ipswich Town

HIGHEST LEAGUE SCORER

Match up the player with the number of goals he scored to finish the club's highest scorer for the season

601.	Andy Gray	2007/2008	27
602.	Andy Gray	2006/2007	20
603.	Ade Akinbiyi	2005/2006	19
604.	Robbie Blake	2004/2005	16
605.	Robbie Blake	2003/2004	11
606.	Gareth Taylor	2002/2003	9
607.	Gareth Taylor	2001/2002	14
608.	Andy Payton	2000/2001	12
609.	Andy Payton	1999/2000	10
610.	Andy Payton	1998/1999	16

STEVE M. DAVIS

611.   Steve was born on 30 October in which year – 1964, 1966 or 1968?

612.   Where was Steve born – Hexham, Wrexham or Padiham?

613.   Steve made his debut for Burnley away on 25 November 1989 against which team?

614.   What was Steve's nickname at Burnley?

615.   How many League appearances did Steve make for Burnley – 317, 327 or 337?

616.   How many League goals did Steve score for The Clarets – 42, 44 or 46?

617.   Which club signed Steve in 1995 for £750,000?

618.   In 1998, again for £750,000 and a record transfer fee at that time, which club signed Steve?

619.   How many League goals did Steve score for The Clarets during 1998/1999 in his 19 appearances?

620.   Steve's last match for Burnley was at Selhurst Park in 2003 against which club?

WHO AM I? – 2

621. I am a Hungarian goalkeeper who signed for The Clarets from Crystal Palace in May 2007.

622. I was born in March 1971, I signed from Bournemouth in February 2000 and I made 115 League appearances for Burnley, scoring 5 goals. I left in 2003.

623. I signed for The Clarets in June 2008 and scored on my League debut, a 4-1 defeat at Sheffield Wednesday on the opening day of the 2008/2009 season.

624. I was the club's highest League scorer with 24 goals during 1996/1997.

625. I am a Norwegian defender who signed for Burnley in June 2008 from Dundee United.

626. I was born in Dublin, I signed for The Clarets from Middlesbrough in July 2001. I made 69 League appearances, scoring 4 goals. I was released in May 2004.

627. I joined Burnley in August 2007 from Preston North End and made my League debut away at Colchester United on 1 September 2007.

628. I managed Burnley between March 1996 and June 1997.

629. I was born in Bolton in October 1980. I signed from Manchester United in July 2003 and left for Wrexham in July 2005.

630. I am a midfielder who signed from Manchester United in July 2008. I scored my first League goal for The Clarets against Preston North End in a 3-1 win during September 2008.

JERRY DAWSON

631. Jerry was born on 18 March in which year – 1888, 1890 or 1892?

632. Just outside of which town was Jerry born – Burnley, Blackburn or Barnsley?

633. Jerry was signed as a full-time professional in February of which year – 1905, 1906 or 1907?

634. For which club did Jerry first play before joining Burnley?

635. Jerry made his Burnley debut on 13 April 1907 in a 3-0 home win against which team?

636. How many League appearances did Jerry make for The Clarets – 512, 522 or 532?

637. True or false: Jerry played in all 42 League games during 1920/1921?

638. What age was Jerry when he made his England debut?

639. Jerry made his last appearance for the club on Christmas Day 1928, aged 40, when they won the match 3-2 against which team?

640. In which year did Jerry retire as a footballer - 1927, 1928 or 1929?

2002/2003

641. Can you name the two players that scored 29 League goals between them during this season, one finishing with 16 goals and the other with 13 goals?

642. True or false: Burnley lost their first four League games?

643. Which team beat Burnley 7-2 at Turf Moor during April 2003, with Robbie Blake scoring a brace for The Clarets?

644. Can you name the two players that scored in the 2-0 home win against Gillingham during April 2003?

645. Who was Burnley's manager during this season?

646. In which position did Burnley finish in the League – 6th, 11th or 16th?

647. Against which team did Burnley record their first League win, in their sixth game of the season during September 2002?

648. Can you name the midfielder that finished the season with 5 League goals during his 28 starts and 5 substitute appearances?

649. Which team beat Burnley 6-5 away from home during October 2002?

650. Following on from the previous question, can you name the two players that scored a brace in the game for Burnley?

GEORGE BEEL

651.   George was born on 26 February in which year – 1888, 1900 or 1902?

652.   From which team did Burnley sign George in April 1923?

653.   George made his Burnley debut on 5 May 1923 at home to which team in a 2-0 defeat?

654.   How many League appearances did George make for Burnley – 306, 316 or 326?

655.   How many League goals did George score during his Burnley career - 179, 189 or 199?

656.   In his nine seasons with The Clarets George scored how many hat-tricks?

657.   How many League goals did George score for Burnley during 1923/1924 in his 34 appearances - 19, 21 or 23?

658.   Which club did George join in 1932 from Burnley?

659.   Against which team did George score a hat-trick on 1 September 1926 in a 5-1 away win?

660.   True or false: George scored 35 goals in 39 League appearances during 1927/1928?

2001/2002

661. How many of their 46 League games did the club win – 21, 31 or 41?

662. Which Greek forward did Burnley sign in July 2001 from Akratitos for £500,000?

663. Who scored a brace in the 5-2 home win against Walsall during September 2001?

664. Can you name the three players that scored against Stockport County in the 3-2 home win during December 2001?

665. In which position did Burnley finish in the League – 7th, 9th or 11th?

666. Who finished as the club's highest League scorer, with 16 goals in his 35 starts and 5 substitute appearances?

667. Which former England international midfielder did Burnley sign from Everton on a free transfer during March 2002, who went on to make a total of 3 starts and 3 substitute appearances during this season and his Burnley career?

668. How many players did Burnley use during the League season – 29, 35 or 41?

669. True or false: the club missed out on the play-off by goal difference, which was only one goal?

670. Who managed The Clarets during this season?

ANDY FARRELL

671. Andy was born on 7 October in which year – 1961, 1963 or 1965?

672. Where was Andy born – Colchester, Ipswich or Norwich?

673. What did Burnley pay to bring Andy to Turf Moor - £10,000, £7,500 or £5,000?

674. From which club did Andy come to Burnley?

675. How many League appearances did Andy make for The Clarets – 227, 257 or 287?

676. How many League goals did Andy score during his Burnley career?

677. Which club did Andy join in September 1994 when he left Turf Moor?

678. How many League goals did Andy score for The Clarets during 1987/1988 in his 45 appearances?

679. Against which team did Andy score Burnley's second goal in the 2-1 home League win on the opening day of the 1988/1989 season?

680. At which non-League club did Andy finish his playing career?

DIVISION TWO CHAMPIONS
– 1972/1973

681. True or false: Burnley won all of their last 6 League matches of the season?

682. What was the club's biggest win of the League season – 4-0, 5-0 or 6-0?

683. Following on from the previous question, which team did they beat during March 1973?

684. Which team did Burnley beat to the title by only 1 point, with the runners-up finishing with 61 points?

685. What was the score when Burnley played Middlesbrough during November 1972 – 2-2, 3-3 or 4-4?

686. Which Midlands team did Burnley beat to record their first League win of the season in August 1972?

687. True or false: Burnley didn't concede a goal during March 1973 in a League game?

688. How many goals did Burnley score in their 42 League matches – 70, 71 or 72?

689. How many of their 42 League matches did the club win?

690. Who managed Burnley to this success?

WHERE DID THEY COME FROM? - 1

Match up the player with the team he came from to join Burnley

691.	Alex Elder	Preston North End
692.	Gabor Kiraly	Celtic
693.	Jack Bruton	Hull City
694.	Tony Morley	Crystal Palace
695.	Keith Newton	Wigan Athletic
696.	Frank Sinclair	Sunderland
697.	Chris Woods	Glentoran
698.	Ian Wright	Everton
699.	David Unsworth	Leicester City
700.	Alan Taylor	Horwich RMI

PETER NOBLE

701. How many League goals did Peter score during his Burnley career – 53, 63 or 73?

702. Which manager handed Peter his Burnley debut?

703. Peter made his Burnley debut in August 1973 away to which team?

704. In which year was Peter born – 1944, 1946 or 1948?

705. How many League goals did Peter score for Burnley during 1978/1979 in 41 appearances, which was his highest goal tally for a season while at Turf Moor?

706. Against which London club did Peter score a brace in a 3-2 home win during April 1975?

707. Which team did Peter sign from to join Burnley?

708. What was Peter's nickname while at Burnley?

709. When Peter left Turf Moor which team did he join in January 1980?

710. Can you name the four managers Peter played under while at Burnley?

WHERE DID THEY COME FROM? – 2

Match up the player with the team he came from to join Burnley

711.	Dean West	Bolton Wanderers
712.	Andy Gray	Bristol City
713.	Brian Jensen	Stoke City
714.	Wayne Entwistle	Glentoran
715.	John Pender	West Bromwich Albion
716.	Wade Elliott	Huddersfield Town
717.	Gordon Cowans	AFC Bournemouth
718.	Nigel Gleghorn	Bury
719.	Glen Little	Sunderland
720.	Sam Wadsworth	Stockport County

ADE AKINBIYI

721.   In which year was Ade born – 1972, 1973 or 1974?

722.   Against which team did Ade make his League debut (first spell) in March 2005?

723.   Following on from the previous question, what happened on his debut – he got sent off, he scored a brace or he got injured after 83 minutes?

724.   Ade moved to which club in January 2006 only to return to Turf Moor in January 2007?

725.   Against which team did Ade score his first Burnley goal during March 2005 in a 2-1 away defeat?

726.   Against which London team did Ade score a brace during a 2-0 home win during April 2005?

727.   How many League goals did Ade score for Burnley during 2007/2008?

728.   Which team paid £5 million for Ade in 2000 in a transfer from Wolves?

729.   Who was the manager who brought Ade to Turf Moor (first spell) in February 2005?

730.   Against which team did Ade score a hat-trick in the Championship during November 2005 in a 3-2 away win?

WHERE DID THEY GO? - 1

Match up the player with the club he joined from Burnley

731.	Roy Stephenson	Leeds United
732.	Willie Donachie	Blackpool
733.	Chris Waddle	Rotherham United
734.	Mike Summerbee	Tranmere Rovers
735.	Stan Ternent	Oldham Athletic
736.	Ian Moore	Birmingham City
737.	Danny Coyne	Sunderland
738.	Terry Cochrane	Carlisle United
739.	Robbie Blake	Torquay United
740.	Bob Kelly	Middlesbrough

PAUL FLETCHER

741.   In which year was Paul born – 1951, 1952 or 1953?

742.   Against which team did Paul make his Burnley debut at home during March 1971?

743.   How many League goals did Paul score for Burnley during 1972/1973?

744.   Which Burnley manager handed Paul his debut?

745.   How many League appearances did Paul make for Burnley in his career - 293, 303 or 313?

746.   Can you name the four managers that Paul played under at Burnley?

747.   In what position did Paul play during his playing days?

748.   How much did Burnley pay Bolton for Paul, then a club record?

749.   How many League goals did Paul score during his Burnley career, in 293 League appearances?

750.   When Paul left Turf Moor for which club did he sign, with Stan Ternent paying £30,000, during February 1980?

WHERE DID THEY GO? – 2

Match up the player with the club he joined from Burnley

751.	Lee Dixon	**Woolwich Arsenal**
752.	Joe Jakub	**Stoke City**
753.	Jimmy Crabtree	**Wolverhampton Wanderers**
754.	Gifton Noel-Williams	**Bury**
755.	Robert Buchanan	**Chester City**
756.	Roger Hansbury	**Real Murcia**
757.	Ray Hankin	**Portsmouth**
758.	Robert McGrory	**Leeds United**
759.	Alec Scott	**Cambridge United**
760.	Malcolm Waldron	**Aston Villa**

2000/2001

761.   In what position did The Clarets finish in the League?

762.   Who was the club's highest League scorer with 9 goals?

763.   Which Greek goalkeeper signed for Burnley during August 2000?

764.   Who was The Clarets' manager during this season?

765.   Who scored Burnley's equaliser on the opening day of the season at The Reebok Stadium in the 1-1 away draw against Bolton Wanderers in August 2000?

766.   Which East Anglian team did Burnley beat 3-2 away from home during April 2001?

767.   Following on from the previous question, can you name the Burnley goalscorers?

768.   Who scored a brace for Burnley in the 2-0 home win against Sheffield United during November 2000?

769.   Who scored a brace for Burnley in the 3-2 away win against Tranmere Rovers during October 2000?

770.   Which striker left Turf Moor in December 2000 and joined Stoke City?

ALAN STEVENSON

771.   Alan was born on 6 November in which year – 1948, 1950 or 1952?

772.   Alan started his football career at which club, famous for producing other top goalkeepers?

773.   Alan made his Burnley debut on 22 January 1972 in a 1-0 defeat away against which team?

774.   How much was Alan's transfer fee to bring him to Turf Moor in 1971?

775.   How many seasons did Alan spend with Burnley?

776.   How many League appearances did Alan make for The Clarets – 418, 428 or 438?

777.   True or false: in the 1980/1981 season Alan only missed two games because he was sent off at Christmas against Blackpool?

778.   True or false: Alan played for England in a full international?

779.   In 1983 which club did Alan move to from Burnley?

780.   True or false: Alan was involved in the Wembley project?

DIVISION FOUR CHAMPIONS
– 1991/1992

781. Who started the season as manager of Burnley and was at Turf Moor until October 1991?

782. Following on from the previous question, which manager took over and led the team to Championship success?

783. True or false: The Clarets lost their first League game of the season?

784. Following on from the previous question, which team did they play?

785. Against which team did Burnley record a 4-1 away win, their first League win during August 1991?

786. Can you name the two teams that also won promotion by finishing 2nd and 3rd in the League table?

787. How many points clear at the top of the League were Burnley when they won the League – 6, 9 or 12?

788. Which team did The Clarets beat 5-0 at home in the League during February 1992?

789. Which Welsh team did Burnley beat 6-2 away from home in the League during October 1991?

790. Who was the clubs top League scorer with 24 goals in 38 games?

SPONSORS

Match up the period with the team's sponsors at that time

791. 1982-83   **Hunters Property Group**
                       (shirt sponsors)

792. 1983-84   **P3 Computers (shirt sponsors)**

793. 1984-88   **Vodka Kick**
                       (away game shirt sponsors)

794. 1988-98   **TheHut.com (short sponsors)**

795. 1998-2000   **Multipart (shirt sponsors)**

796. 2001-04   **TSB (shirt sponsors)**

797. 2003-04   **Holland's Pies (shirt sponsors)**

798. 2004-07   **Poco (shirt sponsors)**

799. 2007-09*   **Endsleigh (shirt sponsors)**

800. 2008-09*   **Lanway (shirt sponsors)**

* Up to the 2008/2009 season

ANSWERS

CLUB HISTORY

1. The Clarets
2. 1882
3. False: 1883
4. The FA Cup
5. True
6. Turf Moor
7. 23
8. Rawtenstall
9. Ian Moore
10. Harry Bradshaw

CLUB RECORDS

11. Jerry Dawson
12. George Beel
13. 2 (1921 and 1960)
14. George Beel
15. Huddersfield Town
16. 1892
17. Jimmy McIlroy
18. 1914
19. Anglo-Scottish Cup
20. Kyle Lafferty

CLUB HONOURS

21.	Division One Champions	1959/1960
22.	Division Three Champions	1981/1982
23.	FA Charity Shield Winners	1973/1974
24.	FA Cup Winners	1913/1914
25.	Division One Runners-up	1961/1962
26.	Division Four Champions	1991/1992
27.	Division Two Champions	1972/1973
28.	FA Cup Runners-up	1946/1947
29.	Pontins League Division Two Champions	1997/1998
30.	Central League Champions	1948/1949

MANAGERS - 1

31.	Frank Casper	1989-91

32.	John Bond	1983-84
33.	Jimmy Adamson	1970-76
34.	Alan Brown	1954-57
35.	Harry Bradshaw	1894-99
36.	Chris Waddle	1997-98
37.	Clive Middlemass	1996
38.	Joe Brown	1976-77
39.	Steve Cotterill	2004-07
40.	Ernest Mangnall	1900-03

NATIONALITIES

41.	Diego Penny	Peruvian
42.	Christian Kalvenes	Norwegian
43.	Steven Caldwell	Scottish
44.	Alan Mahon	Irish Republican
45.	Ade Akinbiyi	Nigerian
46.	Clarke Carlisle	English
47.	Remco Van der Schaaf	Dutch
48.	Kevin McDonald	Scottish
49.	Steve Jones	Northern Irish
50.	Brian Jensen	Danish

MANAGERS – 2

51.	John Haworth	1910-24
52.	Stan Ternent	1998-2004
53.	Harry Potts	1958-70
54.	Frank Hill	1948-54
55.	Adrian Heath	1996-97
56.	Brian Miller	1979-83
57.	Billy Dougall	1957-58
58.	Spen Whittaker	1903-10
59.	Jimmy Mullen	1991-96
60.	Martin Buchan	1985

INTERNATIONALS

61.	Frank Sinclair	28 caps for Jamaica
62.	Alan Mahon	2 caps for Republic of Ireland
63.	Mohammed Camara	79 caps for Guinea

64.	Ian Cox	16 caps for Trinidad and Tobago
65.	Ralph Coates	4 caps for England
66.	Chris Waddle	62 caps for England
67.	Ade Akinbiyi	1 cap for Nigeria
68.	George Brown	9 caps for England
69.	William Donachie	35 caps for Scotland
70.	David Johnson	5 caps for Jamaica

JIMMY ADAMSON

71.	1929
72.	4
73.	1947
74.	True
75.	426
76.	52
77.	False: Jimmy was picked for the England squad for the 1962 World Cup in Chile
78.	Blackpool
79.	4
80.	True

BURNLEY v. PRESTON NORTH END

81.	True: Preston won 2-1 at home and 3-2 at Turf Moor
82.	2-0 to Burnley
83.	Robbie Blake
84.	1971/1972
85.	3-1 to Burnley
86.	2-0 to Burnley
87.	Neill Moore
88.	True
89.	Arthur Gnohere
90.	Ian Moore, Kevin Ball and Glen Little

POSITIONS IN THE FIRST DIVISION

91.	1st with 55 points	1959/1960
92.	14th with 39 points	1969/1970
93.	10th with 42 points	1950/1951
94.	21st with 27 points	1970/1971

95.	3rd with 55 points	1965/1966
96.	6th with 48 points	1952/1953
97.	12th with 42 points	1964/1965
98.	7th with 44 points	1955/1956
99.	15th with 38 points	1948/1949
100.	9th with 44 points	1963/1964

LEAGUE GOALSCORERS - 1

101.	James Adamson	17
102.	Alex Elder	15
103.	Jerry Dawson	0
104.	Brian Miller	29
105.	Kyle Lafferty	10
106.	Willie Irvine	78
107.	Gordon Harris	69
108.	Ray Pointer	118
109.	Ted McMinn	3
110.	Bert Freeman	103

POSITIONS IN THE SECOND DIVISION

111.	21st with 44 points	1982/1983
112.	2nd with 58 points	1946/1947
113.	6th with 44 points	1937/1938
114.	7th with 46 points	1907/1908
115.	19th with 36 points	1932/1933
116.	15th with 37 points	1935/1936
117.	11th with 40 points	1977/1978
118.	1st with 62 points	1972/1973
119.	3rd with 52 points	1911/1912
120.	12th with 41 points	1934/1935

MATCH THE YEAR – 1

121.	Jock Aird made his Burnley home debut in April against Liverpool	1950
122.	Burnley were FA Cup winners	1914
123.	Burnley were Division Three Champions	1982
124.	Barry Kilby joined the board as a director of Burnley	1998

125.	Tony Philliskirk was born	1965
126.	Burnley were European Champions Club Cup quarter-finalists	1961
127.	Gordon Harris was born	1940
128.	John Bond was appointed manager of The Clarets	1983
129.	Endsleigh took over as the club's main sponsor	1988
130.	Burnley were Division Four Champions	1992

FRANK CASPER

131.	1944
132.	False: Barnsley Schoolboys
133.	Rotherham United
134.	£30,000
135.	5
136.	True
137.	237: 230 (7)
138.	74
139.	Cyril Knowles and Norman Hunter
140.	1991

BURNLEY v. BLACKBURN ROVERS

141.	1888
142.	8th attempt (a 3-0 home win during December 1891)
143.	FA Cup
144.	Jimmy Robson
145.	Micah Hyde
146.	2-1
147.	2000/2001
148.	True
149.	2-0 to Burnley
150.	1912/1913

SQUAD NUMBERS 2008-2009

151.	Diego Penny	1
152.	Michael Duff	4
153.	Robbie Blake	20
154.	Gabor Kiraly	17
155.	Clarke Carlisle	5

156.	Wade Elliott	11
157.	Joey Gudjonsson	8
158.	Alan Mahon	18
159.	Brian Jensen	12
160.	Ade Akinbiyi	9

BIG WINS

161.	v. Plymouth Argyle (home), League, April 2007	4-0
162.	v. Norwich City (home), League, April 2007	3-0
163.	v. Watford (home), League, December 2005	4-1
164.	v. Walsall (home), League, September 2001	5-2
165.	v. Wrexham (home), League, November 1999	5-0
166.	v. Colchester United (away), League, October 1998	5-0
167.	v. York City (home), League, January 1998	7-2
168.	v. Gillingham (home), League, December 1996	5-1
169.	v. Peterborough United (home), League, March 1997	4-0
170.	v. Barnet (home), League, April 1994	5-0

HARRY POTTS

171.	1922
172.	True
173.	1946
174.	The General
175.	165
176.	Everton
177.	Shrewsbury Town
178.	True
179.	14
180.	Brian Miller

1970s

181.	17
182.	1972/1973
183.	7th
184.	Tottenham Hotspur
185.	Wolverhampton Wanderers and Sheffield United
186.	15
187.	Jimmy Adamson

188.	6th
189.	True
190.	68: 40 home and 20 away

MARTIN DOBSON

191.	1948
192.	True
193.	Centre forward
194.	Wolverhampton Wanderers
195.	410: 406 (4)
196.	Portugal
197.	5
198.	Everton
199.	£100,000
200.	Bury

STEVE COTTERILL

201.	1964
202.	2004
203.	Cheltenham
204.	Striker
205.	13th
206.	October
207.	Ade Akinbiyi
208.	English
209.	Andy Gray
210.	15th

LEAGUE APPEARANCES

211.	John Angus	438 (1)
212.	Ray Deakin	212 (1)
213.	Adrian Heath	110 (10)
214.	Martin Dobson	406 (4)
215.	Marlon Beresford	286 (1)
216.	Steve Kindon	175 (10)
217.	Ray Pointer	223
218.	Steve M. Davis	321 (6)
219.	Leighton James	331 (5)

| 220. | Ian Moore | 170 (22) |

STAN TERNENT

221. *1946*
222. *Division Two promotion*
223. *1999/2000*
224. *5*
225. *Bristol Rovers*
226. *Andy Payton*
227. *Midfielder*
228. *15th*
229. *2004*
230. *Bury*

JIMMY MCIIROY

231. *1931*
232. *Irish*
233. *Glentoran*
234. *Sunderland*
235. *13*
236. *439*
237. *116*
238. *Stoke City*
239. *55*
240. *Bolton Wanderers*

2007/2008

241. *13th*
242. *Steve Cotterill*
243. *Sheffield Wednesday*
244. *West Bromwich Albion*
245. *Charlton Athletic*
246. *Andy Cole*
247. *Graham Alexander*
248. *Wade Elliott*
249. *Owen Coyle*
250. *Andy Gray*

LEIGHTON JAMES

251.   1953
252.   Swansea
253.   17
254.   Nottingham Forest
255.   336: 331 (5)
256.   Derby County
257.   John Toshack
258.   Czechoslovakia
259.   54
260.   3

BURNLEY v. BLACKPOOL

261.   2-0 to Burnley
262.   Martin Paterson and Graham Alexander
263.   1897
264.   True: 3-1 at home and 2-1 away
265.   The League Cup
266.   3-0 to Burnley
267.   David Eyres and John Francis
268.   Burnley
269.   Graham Branch
270.   Micky Mellon

WHO AM I? – 1

271.   Brian Pilkington
272.   Keith Newton
273.   Gordon Harris
274.   Bob Kelly
275.   Billy Hamilton
276.   Brian O'Neil
277.   Neil Grewcock
278.   Jimmy Robson
279.   Robert Seith
280.   Colin Waldron

1980s

281.   Brian Miller

282.	1981/1982

283.	21

284.	Ian Measham

285.	14th

286.	Martin Buchan

287.	10th

288.	Vince Overson

289.	Norwich City

290.	John Benson

ANDY PAYTON

291.	1967

292.	Huddersfield Town

293.	Bristol Rovers

294.	23

295.	True

296.	156: 115 (41)

297.	69

298.	Grimsby Town

299.	20

300.	Middlesbrough

2006/2007

301.	Queens Park Rangers

302.	Steve Jones

303.	Steven Caldwell

304.	15

305.	Steve Cotterill

306.	Mike Duff, Paul McVeigh, Steve Jones and Wade Elliott

307.	Chris McCann

308.	Norwich City

309.	14

310.	False: 5 wins and 2 defeats

JOHN CONNELLY

311.	1938

312.	St Helens

313.	St Helens Town

314.	20
315.	False: Trevor Meredith scored the winner
316.	215
317.	85
318.	Manchester United
319.	Bury
320.	7

MATCH THE YEAR – 2

321.	Graham Branch signed from Stockport County	1998
322.	Wade Elliott signed for The Clarets from Bournemouth	2005
323.	The club were Division One Runners-up	1962
324.	The club were Division One Champions	1960
325.	Remco Van der Schaaf was born	1979
326.	Clarke Carlisle signed for Burnley from Watford	2007
327.	The club were Division One Champions	1921
328.	The club were FA Cup Runners-up	1947
329.	The club were Division One Runners-up	1920
330.	Diego Penny made his Burnley debut	2008

TOMMY CUMMINGS

331.	1928
332.	Manchester City
333.	Central defence
334.	3
335.	5
336.	434
337.	Bolton Wanderers
338.	Aston Villa
339.	True
340.	None

2008/2009

341.	False: they lost their first two and drew in the third match
342.	Chris Eagles
343.	Joey Gudjonsson, Steven Caldwell and Chris Eagles
344.	Robbie Blake

345.   **Martin Paterson**

346.   **Nottingham Forest**

347.   **Graham Alexander**

348.   **Fulham**

349.   **Wade Elliott**

350.   **Coventry City**

HAT-TRICKS

351.   **Steve Kindon**   *v. Nottingham Forest,*
                                  21 February 1970 (home), 5-0

352.   **Willie Irvine**   *v. Nottingham Forest,*
                                  26 March 1966 (home), 4-1

353.   **Peter McKay**   *v. Portsmouth,*
                                  19 November 1955 (home), 3-0

354.   **Peter Noble**   *v. Middlesbrough,*
                                  30 August 1975 (home), 4-1

355.   **Harry Potts**   *v. Everton,*
                                  3 December 1949 (home), 5-1

356.   **George Beel**   *v. West Ham United,*
                                  17 November 1923 (home), 5-1

357.   **Jimmy Ross**   *v. Leicester Fosse,*
                                  15 January 1898 (home), 4-0

358.   **Louis Page**   *v. Liverpool,*
                                  12 April 1930 (home), 4-1

359.   **Andy Lochhead**   *v. Aston Villa,*
                                  26 November 1966 (home), 4-2

360.   **Bert Freeman**   *v. Fulham,*
                                  2 March 1912 (home), 5-1

OWEN COYLE

361.   **2007**

362.   **Republic of Ireland**

363.   **1966**

364.   **13th**

365.   **Stoke City**

366.   **0-0**

367.   **Striker**

368.   **Airdrieonians**

| 369. | St Johnstone |
| 370. | Columba |

ADAM BLACKLAW

371.	1937
372.	Aberdeen
373.	Goalkeeper
374.	Cardiff City
375.	Alan Brown
376.	318
377.	Blackburn Rovers
378.	Norway
379.	3
380.	1971

LEAGUE GOALSCORERS – 2

381.	Peter Noble	63
382.	Martin Dobson	63
383.	Leighton James	66
384.	John Angus	4
385.	John Connelly	85
386.	Billy Hamilton	58
387.	Adam Blacklaw	0
388.	Ian Wright	4
389.	Andrew Cole	6
390.	John Oster	1

IAN BRITTON

391.	1954
392.	Dundee
393.	10
394.	Torquay United
395.	108: 102 (6)
396.	True
397.	Wolverhampton Wanderers
398.	Scarborough
399.	False: runners-up to Chesterfield
400.	False: he worked in Burnley on the football non-League scene

1990s

401. 5
402. Frank Casper, Jimmy Mullen, Adrian Heath, Chris Waddle and Stan Ternent
403. 13th
404. Southend United
405. Bury
406. 17th
407. Andy Cooke
408. Preston North End
409. 15th
410. Lee Howey

WILLIE IRVINE

411. 1943
412. Irish
413. Arsenal
414. 126: 124 (2)
415. 78
416. Everton
417. Preston North End
418. 8
419. Halifax Town
420. Scunthorpe United

RALPH COATES

421. 1946
422. Leicester City
423. 26
424. 1961
425. Sheffield United
426. Tottenham Hotspur
427. 216: 214 (2)
428. 4
429. 6
430. Leyton Orient

BRIAN MILLER

431. 1937
432. Burnley
433. Defender
434. Chelsea
435. 379
436. 1
437. 29
438. None: Brian only played for Burnley
439. Harry Potts
440. Chief scout

2005/2006

441. Steve Cotterill
442. Mo Camara
443. Ade Akinbiyi
444. James O'Connor
445. Coventry City
446. 17th
447. Andy Gray and Graham Branch
448. Jon Harley
449. Reading and Sheffield United
450. James O'Connor

WHEN WE WERE KNOCKED OUT OF THE FA CUP

451.	13 January 1912, 1st round	Fulham 2-1 Burnley
452.	4 March 1933, 6th round	Burnley 0-1 Manchester City
453.	9 March 2003, 6th round	Watford 2-0 Burnley
454.	16 March 1983, 6th round replay	Sheffield Wednesday 5-0 Burnley
455.	5 May 1962, final	Tottenham Hotspur 3-1 Burnley
456.	29 March 1924, semi-final	Aston Villa 3-0 Burnley
457.	8 March 1952, 6th round	Blackburn Rovers 3-1 Burnley
458.	8 January 2000, 4th round	Coventry City 3-0 Burnley
459.	11 February 1950, 5th round	Arsenal 2-0 Burnley
460.	31 January 1891, 2nd round	Notts County 2-1 Burnley

2004/2005

461.   Micah Hyde

462.   £1.25 million

463.   West Bromwich Albion

464.   False: the club did not quality for the play-offs

465.   10

466.   Danny Coyne

467.   13th

468.   Steve Cotterill

469.   Dean Bowditch, James O'Connor and Jean-Louis Valois

470.   Robbie Blake

RAY POINTER

471.   1936

472.   Luton Town

473.   Centre forward

474.   27

475.   Blackpool

476.   3

477.   223

478.   118

479.   Bury

480.   8

BURNLEY v. BURY

481.   Martin Paterson

482.   3-1 to Burnley

483.   Peter Swan, Paul Smith and David Eyres

484.   Robbie Blake

485.   FA Cup

486.   Andy Cooke

487.   League Cup

488.   3-2 to Burnley

489.   True

490.   Ronnie Jepson

ANDY LOCHHEAD

491.   1941

492.	1958
493.	Manchester City
494.	Chelsea and Bournemouth & Boscombe
495.	Leeds United
496.	226: 225 (1)
497.	101
498.	21
499.	Leicester City and Aston Villa
500.	1968

DIVISION THREE CHAMPIONS – 1981/1982

501.	Alan Stevenson
502.	Brian Miller
503.	Paul McGee
504.	Portsmouth
505.	True
506.	30p
507.	True: Burnley with a plus 21 goal difference and the runners-up with a plus 15 goal difference
508.	Carlisle United
509.	21
510.	Plymouth Argyle

WILLIE MORGAN

511.	1944
512.	Scottish
513.	4
514.	Sheffield Wednesday
515.	Manchester United
516.	196: 195 (1)
517.	19
518.	Manchester United
519.	David Thomas
520.	True

DEBUTS

| 521. | v. Stoke City (home), League, 0-1, January 2007 | Joey Gudjonsson |

522.	v. Sheffield United (home), League, 1-1, August 2004	Mike Duff
523.	v. Sheffield Wednesday (away), League, 1-4, August 2008	Diego Penny
524.	v. Colchester United (away), League, 3-2, September 2007	Graham Alexander
525.	v. Bury (away), League Cup, 2-0, August 2008	Kevin McDonald
526.	v. Scunthorpe United (away), League, 0-2, August 2007	Clarke Carlisle
527.	v. Crewe (away), League, 1-2, August 2005	Wade Elliott
528.	v. Bristol Rovers (away), League, 0-1, January 1998	Andy Payton
529.	v. Walsall (home), League, 0-0, January 1999	Graham Branch
530.	v. Norwich City (home), League, 2-0, November 2000	Ian Moore

DAVID THOMAS

531. 1950
532. 4
533. Everton
534. Don Revie
535. 157: 153 (4)
536. Queens Park Rangers
537. False: QPR were runners-up to Burnley
538. Frank Worthington
539. 8
540. Canada (playing for Vancouver Whitecaps)

LEAGUE GOALSCORERS – 3

541.	Jason Hardy	1
542.	John Spicer	4
543.	Graham Branch	17
544.	Andy Gray	28
545.	Frank Sinclair	1
546.	Richard Chaplow	7

547.	Dean West	5
548.	Mark McGregor	2
549.	Ian Moore	37
550.	John Mullin	10

JOHN ANGUS

551.	1938
552.	1955
553.	Everton
554.	2
555.	439: 438 (1)
556.	4
557.	Arsenal
558.	Austria
559.	None: he only ever played for Burnley
560.	1972

2003/2004

561.	Robbie Blake
562.	Gillingham
563.	19th
564.	Robbie Blake
565.	Luke Chadwick
566.	David May
567.	Graham Branch
568.	Stan Ternent
569.	Ipswich Town
570.	Arthur Gnohere

BRIAN FLYNN

571.	1955
572.	Port Talbot
573.	Neath
574.	Arsenal
575.	202: 193 (9)
576.	Leeds United
577.	Wrexham
578.	3

579. 66

580. 19

UNUSUAL RESULTS

581.	v. Crystal Palace (away), League, May 2008	0-5
582.	v. Plymouth (home), League, April 2007	4-0
583.	v. Cardiff City (home), League, September 2005	3-3
584.	v. Ipswich Town (away), League, October 2003	1-6
585.	v. Preston North End (away), League, December 2003	3-5
586.	v. Norwich City (home), League, April 2004	3-5
587.	v. Grimsby Town (away), League, October 2002	5-6
588.	v. Watford (home), League, April 2003	4-7
589.	v. Sheffield Wednesday (home), League, April 2003	2-7
590.	v. Wrexham (home), League, November 1999	5-0

WHEN WE WERE KNOCKED OUT OF THE LEAGUE CUP

591.	9 October 1984, 2nd round	Burnley 0-3 Manchester United
592.	9 September 1970, 2nd round	Aston Villa 2-0 Burnley
593.	25 September 2007, 3rd round	Burnley 0-1 Portsmouth
594.	5 October 1994, 2nd round	Burnley 1-4 Liverpool
595.	25 October 1977, 3rd round	Burnley 1-2 Ipswich Town
596.	27 August 1991, 1st round	Burnley 2-3 Wigan Athletic
597.	24 September 1997, 2nd round	Stoke City 2-0 Burnley
598.	24 September 1996, 2nd round	Burnley 1-2 Charlton Athletic
599.	6 September 1972, 2nd round	Leeds United 4-0 Burnley
600.	3 December 2002, 4th round	Burnley 0-2 Manchester United

HIGHEST LEAGUE SCORER

601.	Andy Gray	2007/2008	11
602.	Andy Gray	2006/2007	14
603.	Ade Akinbiyi	2005/2006	12
604.	Robbie Blake	2004/2005	10
605.	Robbie Blake	2003/2004	19
606.	Gareth Taylor	2002/2003	16
607.	Gareth Taylor	2001/2002	16

608.	Andy Payton	2000/2001	9
609.	Andy Payton	1999/2000	27
610.	Andy Payton	1998/1999	20

STEVE M. DAVIS

611. 1968

612. Hexham

613. Lincoln City

614. The Skip

615. 327: 321 (6)

616. 42

617. Luton Town

618. Burnley

619. 3

620. Wimbledon

WHO AM I? – 2

621. Gabor Kiraly

622. Ian Cox

623. Martin Paterson

624. Paul Barnes

625. Christian Kalvenes

626. Alan Moore

627. Graham Alexander

628. Adrian Heath

629. Lee Roche

630. Chris Eagles

JERRY DAWSON

631. 1888

632. Burnley

633. 1907

634. Portsmouth Rovers (a team in the Burnley area)

635. Stockport County

636. 522

637. False, he played in 39 games

638. 33

639. Liverpool

640.   *1929*

2002/2003

641.   *Gareth Taylor (16) and Robbie Blake (13)*

642.   *True*

643.   *Sheffield Wednesday*

644.   *Gareth Taylor and Drissa Diallo*

645.   *Stan Ternent*

646.   *16th*

647.   *Derby County*

648.   *Glen Little*

649.   *Grimsby Town*

650.   *Gareth Taylor and Robbie Blake*

GEORGE BEEL

651.   *1900*

652.   *Chesterfield*

653.   *Birmingham*

654.   *316*

655.   *179*

656.   *11*

657.   *19*

658.   *Lincoln City*

659.   *Newcastle United*

660.   *True*

2001/2002

661.   *21*

662.   *Dimi Papadopoulos*

663.   *Lee Briscoe*

664.   *Glen Little, Gareth Taylor and Ian Moore*

665.   *7th*

666.   *Gareth Taylor*

667.   *Paul Gascoigne*

668.   *29*

669.   *True: Norwich City finished with a plus 9 goal difference and Burnley finished with a plus 8 goal difference*

670.   *Stan Ternent*

ANDY FARRELL

671. 1965
672. Colchester
673. £5,000
674. Colchester United
675. 257: 237 (20)
676. 19
677. Wigan Athletic
678. 3
679. Rochdale
680. Leigh RMI

DIVISION TWO CHAMPIONS – 1972/1973

681. False: won 5 and drew 1
682. 4-0 (home win)
683. Portsmouth
684. Queens Park Rangers
685. 3-3
686. Aston Villa
687. False: 5 goals were conceded
688. 72 goals: 44 home and 28 away
689. 24: 13 home and 11 away
690. Jimmy Adamson

WHERE DID THEY COME FROM? - 1

691.	Alex Elder	Glentoran
692.	Gabor Kiraly	Crystal Palace
693.	Jack Bruton	Horwich RMI
694.	Tony Morley	Preston North End
695.	Keith Newton	Everton
696.	Frank Sinclair	Leicester City
697.	Chris Woods	Sunderland
698.	Ian Wright	Celtic
699.	David Unsworth	Wigan Athletic
700.	Alan Taylor	Hull City

PETER NOBLE

701. 63

702. Jimmy Adamson
703. Sheffield United
704. 1944
705. 14
706. Tottenham Hotspur
707. Swindon Town
708. Uwe
709. Blackpool
710. Jimmy Adamson, Joe Brown, Harry Potts and Brian Miller

WHERE DID THEY COME FROM? – 2

711.	Dean West	Bury
712.	Andy Gray	Sunderland
713.	Brian Jensen	West Bromwich Albion
714.	Wayne Entwistle	Bolton Wanderers
715.	John Pender	Bristol City
716.	Wade Elliot	AFC Bournemouth
717.	Gordon Cowans	Stockport County
718.	Nigel Gleghorn	Stoke City
719.	Glen Little	Glentoran
720.	Sam Wadsworth	Huddersfield Town

ADE AKINBIYI

721. 1974
722. Sunderland
723. He got sent off
724. Sheffield United
725. Sheffield United
726. Queens Park Rangers
727. 8
728. Leicester City
729. Steve Cotterill
730. Luton Town

WHERE DID THEY GO? - 1

731.	Roy Stephenson	Rotherham United
732.	Willie Donachie	Oldham Athletic
733.	Chris Waddle	Torquay United

734.	Mike Summerbee	Blackpool
735.	Stan Ternent	Carlisle United
736.	Ian Moore	Leeds United
737.	Danny Coyne	Tranmere Rovers
738.	Terry Cochrane	Middlesbrough
739.	Robbie Blake	Birmingham City
740.	Bob Kelly	Sunderland

PAUL FLETCHER

741.	1951
742.	Southampton
743.	15
744.	Jimmy Adamson
745.	293: 291 (2)
746.	Jimmy Adamson, Joe Brown, Harry Potts and Brian Miller
747.	Centre forward
748.	£60,000
749.	71
750.	Blackpool

WHERE DID THEY GO? – 2

751.	Lee Dixon	Chester City
752.	Joe Jakub	Bury
753.	Jimmy Crabtree	Aston Villa
754.	Gifton Noel-Williams	Real Murcia
755.	Robert Buchanan	Woolwich Arsenal
756.	Roger Hansbury	Cambridge United
757.	Ray Hankin	Leeds United
758.	Robert McGrory	Stoke City
759.	Alec Scott	Wolverhampton Wanderers
760.	Malcolm Waldron	Portsmouth

2000/2001

761.	7th
762.	Andy Payton
763.	Nikolaos Michopoulos
764.	Stan Ternent
765.	Phil Gray

766.   Norwich City

767.   Kevin Ball, Gareth Taylor and Ian Moore

768.   Andy Payton

769.   Steve Davis

770.   Andy Cooke

ALAN STEVENSON

771.   1950

772.   Chesterfield

773.   Orient

774.   £50,000

775.   12

776.   438

777.   True

778.   False: Alan was a substitute against Portugal, but never got a full cap

779.   Rotherham

780.   True

DIVISION FOUR CHAMPIONS – 1991/1992

781.   Frank Casper

782.   Jimmy Mullen

783.   True

784.   Rotherham United

785.   Doncaster Rovers

786.   Rotherham and Mansfield

787.   6: Burnley had 83 points and Rotherham and Mansfield had 77 points

788.   Northampton Town

789.   Wrexham

790.   Mike Conroy

SPONSORS

791.	1982-83	Poco (shirt sponsors)
792.	1983-84	TSB (shirt sponsors)
793.	1984-88	Multipart (shirt sponsors)
794.	1988-98	Endsleigh (shirt sponsors)
795.	1998-2000	P3 Computers (shirt sponsors)

796.	2001-04	*Lanway (shirt sponsors)*
797.	2003-04	*Vodka Kick (away game shirt sponsors)*
798.	2004-07	*Hunters Property Group (shirt sponsors)*
799.	2007-09	*Holland's Pies (shirt sponsors)*
800.	2008-09	*TheHut.com (short sponsors)*

NOTES

NOTES

NOTES

NOTES

NOTES

NOTES

NOTES

NOTES

www.apexpublishing.co.uk